THE TRUE IMPRINT

RAVI KUMAR YADAV

Copyright © Ravi Kumar Yadav
All Rights Reserved.

This book has been published with all efforts taken to make the material error-free after the consent of the author. However, the author and the publisher do not assume and hereby disclaim any liability to any party for any loss, damage, or disruption caused by errors or omissions, whether such errors or omissions result from negligence, accident, or any other cause.

While every effort has been made to avoid any mistake or omission, this publication is being sold on the condition and understanding that neither the author nor the publishers or printers would be liable in any manner to any person by reason of any mistake or omission in this publication or for any action taken or omitted to be taken or advice rendered or accepted on the basis of this work. For any defect in printing or binding the publishers will be liable only to replace the defective copy by another copy of this work then available.

Contents

Contents

Contents

Acknowledgements

The book "The true imprint" is a collection of poetries written by me. All the poems are unique description of the things I see and interpret differently. The poems jotted down in the book are step wise mood changer and depicts how commonly we live but thinking about the same seems weird. I believe nothing is like absurd, just the interpretation matters.

I am profound blissful while presenting my close-to-heart poems. I am immensely grateful to my family and friends, who felt the fire of ambitions of becoming an author. The entire credit of this book goes to them as their motivation and love have always pushed me the entire way. It's my first book and my first effort of parting my thoughts to people through this medium.

I hope you all will enjoy reading.

Prologue

"Poetry becomes the breath, once you fall for it ". Understanding makes them more touching and deep. Every line of the poem is like an embankment under which the deep wells lie. Love for poetry can make your mind compatible with switching to any genre of the poem in the blink of an eye. Poetry is indeed a mood.

Here, in this book, you will get acquainted with the most mood-changing poems. Beginning with a lovely letter to the most depressed people who are just a step before ending their lives, the journey goes ahead illustrating what the soul exactly desires. Love is the sky, its vastness can neither be described nor measured. Love succeeds if interpreted right else love is a failing subject. Understanding love is like hearing the sound of a stone thrown in the ocean. Further, we seem to be independent yet somewhere we are acting on someone's vision and order. We are puppets with invisible controlling threads. In 'Un-traced reproach", it becomes clear how reproach or critics remain invisible yet affect our lives largely. A person is mortal but his doings turn immortal if done for others' sake, this has been depicted beautifully and very shortly in the poem "Life beyond death". The world is a crowd of good and bad. No one prays for the victory of bad yet they turn out to be betrayals, as portrayed in " the world of betrayals". In such an evil surrounding, caning the wicked fellowship and careless nurture, the one who resumes shining with originality is the best spirit. Seeking the values both virtual and tangible as granted, we have inflamed all the respect and honor for those people in whose life's envelope lies the credit of bestowing these. Moreover with time, every moral has been reduced to cinders in the fire of accentuation. You will get a better picture of it in the poem "Cinders in flame". In "The power of love" you will get a deep insight into the complications of love that binds the highest mountains to the deepest trenches. The man tired and sick of all the complexities and struggles of his life has lost all his patience and instead of pleasing with words, he yells out like a storm in hell about all the ailments that he has been facing in this world and further pleads in a threatening way. This seems interesting and relatable. To get into what he requests, " a threatening request" offers the space. Is the world limited to what our eyes see? Well, the concept of dreams and hallucinations resists this. Despite noticing and making large descriptions of my interpretation of the world and its people, I failed in understanding their changing nature with the era. I, thus, blame myself for such a quixotic and wrong analysis. However, my wrong interpretation does not mean I am a bad soul. My rough words out of frustration ruined my life and led me to a lonely life again. So every day is marked by my painful tears asking my beloved that there is no sorry to die. Some people might think of themselves as being loaded on someone's shoulder and sadly but hopefully they believe that their going far can help in saving a hundred lives. He is a double-faced man, a common but dark truth. If hit the golden person, this statement would fall off its weight. But in the poem " That double-faced man", you would get that the statement still holds weight if spoken or heard by a person of independent thoughts. Love can turn everything possible. It's a question for boys - what's the present you would gift your beloved for proving your love? And girls - what grand gift would you ask for to get a hint of how much he loves you? Honestly love doesn't need any explanation or proof. But the truth is people go for it. Thus presenting you the poem " Gifting you the sun", which singles would find humorous because of the kind of gift the man chooses, at the same time, couples would find it romantic and would yearn and expect the same kind of love. Love can fulfill you and complement your empty part but once you are broken in a relationship, be the cause of any, the agony of solitude hovers around you and makes you feel low and heavy. That's because you expected a mountain of love and care and he or she just pushed you off the cliff. A broken heart is the toughest thing to deal with. Life is full of pulls and pushes where at many times you would feel to just surrender your life or would take a step to end up it. We can never count the number of moments in our life where we were dealing with both physical and mental death yet, at last when the last suicide is committed out of knotted thoughts, nobody can pull you out of death well. The dreadful situations, where even your heart starts skipping its beats, life murders you painlessly making you cold to hinder your fighting capacity. 'Painless Murder' illustrates this. The song of loneliness is even sung in the crowd. Alone, the term that is itself so lonely, has innumerable complaints and predictions. Death is the truth like the rising of the sun from the east. Yet it deeply shakes the people surrounding someone who meets death. It's, indeed, a deal of life. The pain of death dies with the dead and hence, only the pain and grief of his family and friends are known and witnessed. Sometimes, the death of a beloved one is too harsh and tough to accept. Within the polluted and complex lifestyle, we have forgotten what the term pleasure means. Nature, the kindest, has within itself numerous melodies that one would never get bored of. Moreover, it's the most precious and prestigious gift that living beings have been bestowed with. In the poem "The serene melody of nature" you would catch a better insight into how nature heals all physical and mental injuries. There are few people, whom you will rarely find, who leave no reason to love themselves. For them, their interests and favorites are the priorities. The same is depicted in the poem 'Left no reason. That's an epic one" How I wanna call my death? Some circumstances and choices take away the shine of life because ultimately, those choices have the root connection to your future and more elaborately your entire life. Love and affairs have become the air today. Therefore it is natural for me to suspect that in this crowd I am losing my trusted love. Every journey starts with a cry and ends with a smile but only if tackled all the hurdles efficiently. When one fails to handle or face trouble, he does the same as described in the poem In the middle of the lane. It takes a longer to know what each line of the poem means yet reading these immensely touches the soul and pleases our mood. The suspense of the meaning makes the poems more exciting and deep. Moreover, the book has started with a poem very dear to life, which will make you realize the unwavering worth of life. Then there is a choice that you make to further pave the way for your life "Mind or mountain". No beauty is imperfect rather imperfection lies in how we treat that. The effort is never less if exerted to get beyond the old self. But the circumstance of our society plays an obverse role for the female gender who in return take the restrictions as their fate. Nobody exactly knows at the beginning of their life why they listen to others and act accordingly because we take their orders as granted. And after realizing that we had no existence of our own identity, our regret burns us alive. What makes us smile today would make tears in the last phase of our life when our idle mind memorizes all the past events. When we imagine ourselves to be of some kind, we start making its vibe all along our thoughts and hence our dreams make us meet ourselves. Believe it or not, your smile and hope to relish whatever kind of life you are living, can push away the darkness of your death. To live life breathe the innermost essence of you. The moral jewels are shared when one understands what is eating away the inner essence of the other. Hope and optimism are such jewels to be shared without worrying about their value. Those with the most stable place in the biosphere are claimed soulless by us. We harm them mercilessly without considering their importance. Some gems make the best of the worst. They are the sweat earner. For them, sweat is the measure of their existence. Isn't it weird that the presence of the things you missed on the ground is found after your death? The parallelly distanced stars above the pensive mind console the loneliness, perfectly described in the poem " The star and me". Somewhere between the darkness, the thoughts may sway like the mermaid of a dreamy emerald sea. Countering the dazzlingfake glitter, those in vague view are of faithful value. I hope you would love reading the poems.

About The Author

**"Spills could hear your heart out and so does the tides spills quietly make a listen while tides tend to react"**

Ravi kumar yadav is the author of "The true imprint: a glance beyond sky".Presently, he is a lecturer in Jharkhand government with additional in-charge of Principal. He wrote the book during his working days. He is vehemently fond of penning down his words to weave a poetry. His additional areas of interest are singing, story writing, traveling and obviously teaching.

1. Dearly to suicides

He committed suicide
The family excruciated the loss
Some cursed the boy's fear
While few were prompted to escape life toss
For those few, life ahead became drudgery
Kept choice - either would be done or will die
Better than struggling, closing life's chapter seemed easy
And they finally choose escaping to sky
Leaving behind their innocent families
And the approaching good days after tough road
For biding away the mental unrest
With open arms, heaven's cart they board
Finally a trend and cycle of suicides
Rampant to turn out the sphere
Spreading terror far and wide
Others pretending " The air from somewhere. "
So my dear future suiciders
Don't deal your life in seconds nine
Cause your moms bore pain for months
To heartily hug you and say ' Oh! dear child mine'
I know struggles of life are back breaking and heart
sinking
But these are meant to fight

Not to sit lonely in dark preparing suicidal note
And fear till jumping from height
Please my dear friends
Think a dozen times before indulging in such act
You may take away your soul but leave behind many
Who will immensely shed tears beating breast intact.

2. Want of soul

It's world
Nothing is going to last long
In this universe
Disaster has its own wreak
And we,
The tongue slippers for numerous dislikes
The action seekers possessing innumerable mistakes
The head frustrating overtime
The mind thinking beyond the reality
And eyes still expecting one's real or fake fame
Aren't out of the world
Our soul needs space
Where love forgives all flaws
And motivates for relishing the rest life
Relishing life is not restricted, not confined
And encouraging enough to regretting minds
Opening the door to dive beyond the ocean.

3. Interpretation of deep love

One day I woke up and found you beside me
So I started saying all the hoarding inside me
"well, the last night I had cried equal to lake"
and also explained that the words I said were not at all fake
So baby , I began from your beauty
thinking it to be an "ideal boyfriend's duty"
and I shifted towards my words healings
that gave me a platform to express my feelings
<u>So I began again like -</u>
Oh! my dear, empress of my heart
How can I stay alive on being apart ?
You have kept me awake from all the sleep
Isn't this what my love for you deep ?
<u>She replied me blushing -</u>
My dear Adam, you are the first citizen of my heart
even I would die on being apart
But I am sorry to say that I had a nice sleep
So can't this be measured as my love deep ?
<u>And she gave a big pause to speak</u>
<u>Maybe she thought speaking out all could make our relation weak</u>

<u>So I continued again, breaking the ice -</u>
"When I think about you, I simply forget myself"
and your words helped me work like the magical elf
Also, when you ignored me, it made me weep
So, do become mine forever 'cause I love you so deep
<u>She was hearing me all silent</u>
<u>About her praises and rudeness without turning violent</u>
<u>So I carried on -</u>
My love! by the grace of God I got you
and thanks for filling my life with so attractive hue
Your anger always gave my cheeks lots of tears to seep
Why are you silent dear, approve all there as my love deep
?"
<u>So, she ultimately opened the shutter</u>
<u>and to the following words she did utter -</u>
Oh dear! I seek for pardon, but I really didn't weep
Nor ever gave tears to my cheeks so that they seep
However I have lots of promises and will surely keep!
So now please approve this proposal as my love deep.
Hearing these words, I was hot with fire
I simply cursed her and titled her as a 'love liar'
And before I could say her another word
I was up by the door ring that I heard
Later, I realized that I was on my bed
Watching the dream all inside of my head
and the very moment, I took decision and stood up with
all my force

to go to her and give her our "relational divorce"
Without any argument, She signed our imaginary divorce
file
and gave me divorce, making a face with cheerless smile
For I thought the best way to express love was my love
definition
So I dumped her just for an imagination
And today I am alone, making my death stake
for she was correct and my thoughtless decision was the
biggest mistake
Also, today after so many taunts and rejection
I feel that I should have meant her love definition
I feel sorry for I never knew that the love mountain was so
steep
and also because I failed understanding the real essence of
the love deep !

4. The suicidal control

I was a puppet, puppet on this earth
I was made with surrounding's talks and
it was false that my mom gave me birth
'cause when I wanted to climb the tree,
its branches were cut
When I wanted to see the surrounding through windows
its glasses were shut,
When I wanted to get on terrace ,
the ladders were misplaced
And when I wanted to wear sneakers
I was given bellies which were already tied and laced!
It was all because I was a puppet, puppet on this land
and my strings were not with my parents but
with the surrounding's hand!
My wings were cut,
when I wanted to fly
My tears were forcefully wiped,
When I wanted to cry
My pillow was snatched,
When I wanted to sleep
And I was called an actress,
When I felt to weep!
It was all for I was a puppet, puppet in the society

And I was made in the way they wanted to make me
treating me like a rubbish doll brutally.
Yes, I was tied up in the society's chain
and was forced to walk in the lamb's lane!!

5. Society and me

Well! I was new to this world
And too young to know the term "society"
I thought it wasn't mandate but
Their vision always held me guilty
For my every action
I had to be accountable
For their choices and faves
I sacrificed all I was capable
I was made to behave
As per their gender based stereotype
Or else threatened or harassed emotionally
For getting a societal wipe
No matter what I was fond of
Their reaction was forever on priority
How awful they'll talk of myself
If I consider my anything pretty
I was of belief: the world is my family
And a great source to support
But true acquaintance was marked
When parents told me their deeds of all sort
But I am never gonna be their subject
Would rather break their prejudices
To let the future, not suffer, to accomplish

Their exuberant wishes!

6. Untraced reproach

She wished for wings
They gave her rope
She needed support
They destroyed her hope
She, enough potential
Looked for scope
Nobody was ready
To part their cope
She herself tried climbing a cliff
They pushed her off slope
Now they sit to curse her
for she hung herself with the rope!

7. Love beneath chapters

Love was never transparent
It was always a shy worm
That eats away your judgements
And lends you purity for someone
Love isn't the venus alone
It lies in its shine out of love for self indeed
And even if there was no rings
Saturn would never forget the warmth of their presence
Love is known as scars with which the moon proudly
shines
And even if it was meant a fall
Love was the coming spring
In the green wide meadows
Every burnt paper was white
And every phase of moon is bright
Love is lovely and indeed a bond
That is unconditional, unwavering
And undoubtedly unquestioning.

8. World of betrayals

The world, a liar
A betraying buddy
Tells and teaches lie
Just to keep others in custody
Indifferent to others life
Who contending for their rights
No morals knock their minds
Persist with their dross fights
Love of life is drudgery
For them the best is revenge
Other's sufferings and injuries
To their mindset, fails to change
A vast sea of humanity
Lacks the trustworthy
Their deception and ignorance
Makes their heart swarthy

9. The best spirit

Lost in the betrayal
of darkened heart
The best spirit
Lost its frenzied part
Indifferent to the poor's feed
Treacherously making others mutt
Thinks everyone as their slave
Brainless, steel tendon robutt
Just pants on shudder
Thinks the life a perpetuating bubble
I feel they're too hideous
For exhausting others in trouble
Enough's enough but
Feels nice on other's shrieks
Own groaning are served
For others, have brutal, ruthless tricks
Their words quiver persist
Nitwatness loses in the mist
I feel ,God ! what a shuddering life
Fails to balance on the tones of Fife

10. Cinders in flame

The life is relentless
and full of hardships
The life simply means
a slender keeps
Pretty hideous it becomes when
danger comes to a man
his courage cinders in flame
and thinks of elation which can
The honesty cinders in flame
when all becomes a blackguard
and immensely shake the goodness
which was left too hard
Infernal deeds of a crazy
impertinence words of imposters
cinders the fraternity in flame
lending persistence to divisions by ancestors

11. The power of love

"Life then death"
is the pure slogan
but "died to live"
looks perplexing and fun
The relentless life goes on
its the common humdrum
but love and loving ones
gives the best on being sum
Love has a dexterous mystery
Even the lost one frantically gets victory
the loving heart spreads far
though gingerly on the obstinate bar
The contours of love
echoes on hill
and its power propels
with pitches and shrill...

12. A threatening request

Hey! The Passing you
Just turn the side invisible to you
Here I am shouting strangely
A wild cry that you would just feel
And you'll feel like calling a crowd
The crowd, you know
For not softening my wounds
But to display all, like a show
A wild request that may seem like a threat
Just bind me in shackles
And turn me behind bars
But do donate me a visible side
A visible corner to sit
To sit and cry with bloody tears
And exhibit my lamentable sacrifice
The sacrifice that yearns for satisfaction
And liberation contently
Behind bars I'll yelling unworldly phrases
That won't affect you but express me
My pitiful lamentation within
That the world failed to feel
And I'd liberate unknowingly

13. The hallucination

She was staring at me
With those frightful red eyes
that may have lost innumerable days of sleep
The most serrated sharped teeth ever
I witnessed the most ugly and odious face
and the sudden of her appearance
O God ! I jumped a feet off my bed
falling in the murk of my room
She was about to take away my breathe
and the terrible intolerable shout she roared
The rough blows were choking my neck
and I turned unconscious out of trepidation
With the horrifying dusty storm she started approaching
me
and I panic-stricken predicted for no life the another
second
And now that she was the closest to me
her flash broke my tone
and I opened my eyes paining in death
I could feel the scars of scare
but could find no such scene
All that I wildly saw
Was the power of dream

Yet I conquered it and am alive
To look for the another hallucination

14. I was wrong

Passing three decades of my lifespan
Even now am not experienced to recognize a man
I had believed on his every tricky act
and trusted his every words like fact
His tears are enough to mark him right
Wait, 'I witnessed he himself had started the fight'
For such black hearts, the justice is unjust
For him his possessions possess priority first
Their is an evil behind every pretty face
Every corrupt is a winner in the worldly race
There is wickedness behind every tear
Beneath many mind opening lectures, there are thoughts
mere
Here, no lotus rises out of mud
but sighs of relief for hiding faults shedding blood
Game of emotions is marked as life
No apologies for mistakes but a suicidal note with knife
Every sweet word hides roughness of the taste
Escaping his guilts, every fake emotions are off like waste
I, the victim of the hypocratic natured being
have ruined my beliefs of everything
Now that I remember the memories of my old days
I say, "I was wrong analyzing his vivid cheating ways."

15. Sorry to die

My whole heart, open the door
Ok, I accept and am strongly repenting
Please open the door
I am impatiently waiting
I am sorry, my love
for the morning fight
I am restlessly waiting
to hug you tight
Please open your eyes
Please make an effort to come out
Please Oh darling, leave your anger
Please try to hear my shout
I am holding my ear
am sitting on my knees
Please oh dear, open your eyes
Make an effort! please
Titillate my head
and wipe off my tear
convince my dead soul
Make an effort dear
You can't go away
leaving me alone
You can't watch silently

my heart-melting moan
Dear, you had promised
We'll take off together
How can you cheat me?
by early raising of your feather
How can you leave me?
to sit lonely in corner to cry
and you wrote sorry in your hand
dear, there is no ' Sorry to die'

16. Saving a hundred lives

He left for dark leaving the light
Stood for alms leaving the castle
He had learnt every step is one's own
He chosen going far from all his known
Cause his perceptions went ahead
Pondering"I may be a force"
My preferences may be a pain
For those very close to me.
His choices could hurt the knowns
His words could hit the knowns
His actions could tense the knowns
His reactions could kill the knowns
So came up with one way
He left all and walked away
Saving a hundred lives.........

17. That double faced man

I was lonely walking at night
A little afraid, yes right
For every step I watched all side
One way relief, I had no one to be abide.
My house was at far
I could hitch no buses or car
For my scaring eyes, the distance increased
I walked roughly on the road greased
I had a bag with phone inside
But I couldn't call for the battery had died
I preferred walking fast with silence
Cause dark had 'to hinder and scare' license
It wasn't cold but I felt cool
Suddenly I saw a man near the school
He looked terrifying with moustache till cheeks
While I was stepping, he gave peeks
I could feel tense in my mind
Then he started approaching me from behind
I tried walking faster without turning back
A heaviness on my shoulder, I saw a hand black
His masked face, dull and dark
The night more horrified with dogs bark
I forgot the words out of fear

All seemed blur in my eyes full of tears
Before I did take another step
He asked, "May I help?"
I was a bit relaxed to say
"No I will walk my own way."
"By the way don't try to chase!"
" Who knows where you'll change your phase"
"Oh! Dear girl, I am a man of grace"
"See my heart, don't visit my face"
" I'll be at far, and will shield"
"And take you safely across the field"
"How can I trust a stranger and especially a man"
"It's up to you, if you want you can"
I took his grace and walked all together
At that moment I was a bird ready with feather
Fortunately, with his mercy I was at my house
All right, in front of my guiding spouse
His face unveiled at the time
Giving my thoughts a boost sublime.

18. Gifting you the sun

My love, you know
You mean me my whole
Cherishing all your lovely moments
I would satisfy my soul....
For you my darling
I would collect the reasons to smile
And bestow you the events of your choice
To adore your happiness all that while.....
My dearie, with a grand welcome
I would breathe you in
And dote on all your imperfect perfections
Holding in my hand your beautiful chin.....
And snapping your best shots
With all your alluring poses done
I would shower you with all the radiance
While gifting you the splendid sun

19. The agony of solitude

I read and tagged for a while
To lose his memories I travelled a mile
Neither I could rage nor weep
Even my painful eyes refused to sleep
Mind got blocked and heart fell ill
For it needed nothing more to get kill
No recreation worked a bit
My pain could call no medical kit
This hearty wound, deeper than vale
I could be relieved by no tale
Though foody but hardly I could eat
And this heart started skipping the beat
My breath was full of sorrow
Hope denies for his comeback tomorrow
I lost aquaintance to my emotions
And my broken tears could be healed by no lotions
Completely overwhelmed by solitude
Now sitting heavily with hands nude
He left my hand and it became load
Regret left me with no lively mode
Nothing left, I feel to suicide
No responsibility left to be abide
Tears have not forgotten their way

Corner of my eyes; their abode to stay
Now dark seems my only mate
For him now I am a subject of hate
Now his every memory will turn me bony
I wish death to hug me and my agony....

20. The last suicide

I led a several lives
You know, all with healing hope
The reason,
I would never understand
Cause I've led the last suicide
Hope, fate, desire and soul
All stood sulking unknowingly
The reason,
I would never understand
Cause I've led the last suicide
One cured with shinning eyes
Second time, the luck awaited
But again and again I broke within
All hope became hopeless
The way, I had to go on
I strangely stepped back
And where the cliff ended sharply
I strongly stepped ahead
The last thing I perceived
"I won't get back from this well"
For all your help, my angles
I am heading towards hell
The reason, I would never understand

Cause I've led the last suicide......

21. A painless murder

I was murdered a dozen times
All that was painless
But enough to darken my mind
And squeeze my red heart
He held the whip but cursed me
And the unused whip lost its hit
He opened fire but I wasn't burnt
Though felt the extremest heat
Surrounded by icebergs I got no frostbite
But my heart was trapped in ice
He ruined my lovely made world
And I was broken within
He took away my relatives though I was not harmed
But rooted out my reason to live
No bruises, no bleeding, I was safe and alive
Though was alone with my mistakes and regrets
I was murdered a dozen times!!!!!!

22. Alone

I would wail looking at sky

to let my cry reach too high

and call the clouds upon to rain

to furnish a rainbow to my pain

My tears would let the flowers to bloom

enchanting fragrance to spread in my room

I wouldn't let anyone to close the door

to let the spray flourish more

The dirt of my hardworking hand

would ask for no abode on land

it will love to be flowed

and weariness vanish in the air blowed

The rising hope in grasses spry

I won't let them hear my cry

I would rather hug a tree

to let my despaired mind be free

I wish no love to be showered on me

for unlocking my expression I would offer no key

I would lie on grass green

everyday to mark the stars as seen

I don't expect to be fed by spoon

and would sing no lovely rhyme for moon

its shattered image behind the trees

will bestow my fire cool breeze
If I would feel to sing a song
I would approach the forest throng
if my heart sinks in thoughts deep
I would distract it with a loud beep
I wouldn't let butterflies to sprinkle me charm
I would simply queue them next and cause no harm
Now I won't have bookmarks of memories to be cherished
I'll be too far to let you know that I have perished
You know I wouldn't let anyone to blame
from my life to rub off your name
only I would tell you I choose darkness to moan
and now nature is little mine for you left me alone.....

23. Death : a deal of life

The wounds of death
though are alive,
is treated as a ceremony
for liberation of elements five.
The body burns in fire
but its works are essence of air
past, present and future inculcated
chances to remember are uncertain and unfair
Every beautiful moment of life
rests in scenario out of smoke
and the bad ones experienced
fall on ground as ash, the earth shook
His good works are message
to the world insane out of greed
and the one committed out of evil
propels within people for selfish feed
The belongings are then the earth's waste
for no museum exists for unique men
his sufferings and devotions are laid
for his immortal journey, humans have no plan
Pain may be excruciating for his family
but does not forever persist
In front of lamentation of his death

mist out the fact "light comes out of mist".

24. The serene melody of nature

The golden air without hits
Slightly moving over the head
Only the chirp of the wagtail
And the shrilly cicadas
Lying in the shade, I
Jocundly of the tree
Which sheds leaves as for love
And makes my pensive mind free
The lake along the untenured fence
Merrily flowing on gentle slope
And the seedlings nearby
Rise as the ray of hope
The above clouds float a brake
For an angel to come down♀?
To make me sleep
Without tensions on crown
This serene melody of nature
Is opulent of height
And the peace it bestows mesmerizes
At several of eye- catchy sight

25. Left no reason

When you'll meet her
You'll find a satisfied soul
Cause she left no reason
Not a mark of any depression or hole
She was the happiest of all
Cause her love was 'she'
She cared herself and her every choice
Pinned up everything that made her glee
She beautified her garden with flowers
And cooked a wide ,to eat
She was pleased talking to herself
And ardently offered herself the seat
Standing a fore, she asked the mirror
To choose, for her, the best dress
With every sun, she furnished a rose
To herself to impress
Laying merrily under blue sky
She chosen the brightest star
With her eyes slightly closed
She built fantasy so far
She gifted herself every birthday
The crown of radiance leveling up
And she tightly hugged herself

Every time she got a hiccup

It's not that she hated the world

But wanted an honest life without

About the world's dishonesty, hatred and violence

Very early, she had heard a man's shout

She wasn't alone, had befriended the nature

Surrounded by birds, flowers, sky and trees

Every memory that she snapped

Cherished her and her friends' cheese

Now that she's no more alive

Still her coffin is the most serene

In the darkest, terrifying graveyard

Nature bestowed her the loveliest scene....

26. How I wanna call death??

I won't urge you to silently and peacefully make me fall
I won't either insist you to take me away painlessly
Dear death, my only friend, to whom my entity is the last
I would never request your to hug me warmly
I have befriended you and indeed it was the record of fate
Yet I won't die to fall in you dark lap
You'll will accurately present to see me passing away
Hey my bestie, don't be tensed, in fact I would meet you
the way you want
With your desires at priority, I would breathe my last
breath
All that I would wish for is being isolated at the end of my
chapter
So I won't hurt the upcoming days of the new lives
You are most welcome, I would definitely wait to meet
you at time right
And as willing for long, would sit alone on corner readily
To meet you enthusiastically and wave a good bye
To this true and real role of the show
I would love my death and interim would mark no
wailing of bereavement.....
Indeed a serene death

27. The shine to the dark

Being sandwiched for being single or not
I possessed no experience of mine
Where I enjoyed the laziness of singularity
Hope for a partner led me lose shine
A late sleep, indeed no tension
A warm sleep missing her arm
Lately awaken nobody to worry or scream
Hugging teddy to adore her charm
Fortunate to relish all the delicacies alone
Interim without a partner, all turns insipid
Half percent still balancing both weights
Still consoling myself to turn to examine experience vivid
Turning now to watching a movie
Romantic ones yearns for her Presence
And horror movies make need of her tight hug
Yet when single am not worried for extra expense
With her around, surrounding would be aromatic
Though singularity would capture no under cause
So have been doubting my future to be
Of befriended one, would I repent for what the past was
Am in fact a struggling man
Caught in the exclusive cage of dilemma and doubt
Am not in way of ruining the lives ahead

Cause it's life, not what the story was about

In fact a sin would weight my head

If I turn wild on her little tender heart

I am indeed unsure what I truly long and need

As the time of building up future has pushed a start..

I am happy right now

Once glad, the other moment weep, they bark

Am unsatisfied whether my fragile option

Would push my shine to dark...

28. If losing trusted love

Love being the most influential
I am afraid of withholding the same
Well not in touch now, am solitude
Cause for betrayal, I can't just turn to blame
Still unveiling my innermost feeling
To know myself better before I fall
Am still unknown to the person I'll love a lot
Because love isn't a just feeling at all
Making myself comfortable with the person
I would wish to share my whole
Embodying- love isn't just between bodies
But too is the emotional connection of the soul
Have heard of many stories
People die loving the one who never knows
I wish within my circle there's nobody such
Cause I wish no unintentional hurt to those
Among the crowd, I have been so fading
Of the story I have heard, whether is applying itself in me
I would rather hug that person
For carrying this heavy feelings sea
Or else if known from otherwise
I would end up curtailing my mind
Though unknowingly but hurting the one

Who has been in role of such kind

29. In the middle of lane

Heart broken, eyes intoxicated
And mind determined to suicide
Words hid inside and face full of tears
Nobody there against this decide
I was meant to stand till death
With the speedy train approaching soon
In the night, likely to fall as corpse
To shine deadly in the bloody moon
Hope now left for the train only
To cut me apart and forgive my fear
In the daylight however, I took no chance
In the crowd to ridiculously appear
They would deride on saving my risk
Layering me with another reason
Making me more insane to die close
Waiting for no change in season
Suicide is my proclivity
They fail to understand this
In their eyes, my weakness is pulling me
Lending me no space of bliss
Particularly to escape I opted this path
In the whole sea of darkness
They were seeking for trace of wrath

I was still unknown to their mere politics

'Was still being full of regret to spread this dare

But they wanted it to happen or to save

To laugh at unleashing expectation of care

With trembling legs, I stood chest a front

To lose myself to the air at short

Would now look for no dream

To confirm my will of death; abort

And as I'll escape to sky

I would never see down to earth

At no condition I would risk again

To here as a man take another birth...

30. Striving for a pleasing day

I was tapering for the last pleasure
I thought of having my ambitions measure
To those who have relished life
Having described it as melodious as fife
And looking at them I was heedless to mine sad days
And no wonder, out of such feel, I was seeking for the ways
Yet I could not find one
For me the mixture always was separated like swan
When I looked at grass, they were spry though small
But this little motivation was not all
I moved to nature to see if God was really great
Biting my fingers, I began to sweat
And I, from then was allegiant to his art
By bestowing niche to all those part
And as I observed his love so invisible yet vast
And poor me was wailing for that gone in past
I was yet to kindle high
Cause my age was not a matter to shy
Book of life has similar pages till end
And how I write it would give it a sharp blend
I had no reason to console this freak

I was now no more a weak

31. Love in matter of words

Every bangle tinkling with grace
has broken beating upon the face
Those eyes carrying sparkle of hope
now stone-heartedly bearing the hazard to cope
such sight has turned waiting impatiently unending
forcing hearts to voice cries most excruciating
jewels that used to adorn the celebration of his presence
have been faded out of his true essence
waiting to hug him tightly after a long
rather mercilessly pushed to bid goodbye the rest life long
Every letter that frantically pleaded for his return
has been spilled in ink to mourn
she agonizing when world prayed and praised his valour
now dispelled from beauty like a wandering sailor
"once, just once open eyes to inform about the go"
deadly infront of posthumously body, she made her last
bow
"fires of your pyre flourishing for your courage high"
melting the soul within me, flaming my life in ashes to
sky

32. Bad in hate the same out

I'm a bit over thinker
Of my past beating it dark
And indeed every few hours
I would do the most unwanted cry
Full of tears of repent
Watching the horrific scene
Of the rapid time walk
Giving me no time to get breathe
Of the moment I lived and will live
However, my nostalgia
Hates the wailings of out
Introverted till the extended age
Of my air like life
I'd sit once to count the days
And aware myself of the remaining part
To rise below the sun

33. Painting my dream

The black to get cover of sky
The green though dark to depict nature
Yes I had the beauty of depth
And a light hand so warm in look
Even more convincing to my parched soul
And I saw myself running blindly
As if a chase to someone I lost
A note in my hand, my hand in air
And the air so luke on my yearn
The run so rapid leaving drops of tears
Making my every single thought a milestone
And so soothing so warm and so healing
The same hand I felt back
Even the water from clouds
Could quench thirst of my throat and not heart
So sitting down a mysterious tree
With graceful branches and non rustling leaves
And a magical lake nearby where instead of fishes
The dead desires floated with the curvy waves
And the time, the perfect one
To let me think of finding out my one
My drawing paper left blank

34. The imprints of my scars

That night ,
I fought my sadness
I fought my pain
I fought my anxiety
I fought my depression
I fought my doubt
I fought my criticisms
I fought my limitations
I fought my fears
The next day,
I found my body
With the imprints of my scars

35. We know the truth

They made it to cheat intentionally
And accentuated it naturally occurred
They turned to twice their craze
And harassed the other for right
They killed the bird with triggering words
And held it suicide undistinguished
They sang for the goodness, oh no,
But to gain attention of unwanted sympathy
Still the truth we write
Cannot be foretold with boldness in crowd
But staying in weaved huge layered shell
Because one knows the right
And the wrong has defence tight

36. Hope that seems hopeless

I admired how the darkened Sun
Again shines with hope that dies
I made myself a bit to it
But devastating were my inner cries
I admired birds that flew with freedom
And height above all reach
Yet when I turned to their full hope
They soon leave at night for the darkest teach
And yet am going to gain a little peak
To the nature that seems so hopeful
Unlike what my mind predicted
Everything turns downtrodden with dark and dead

37. Years

All this era meant to burn me
Heat me up and never
To my belief a warm up
I have been through long years
Of unjustified wars
Mockingly lying behind the doors
Means to the future me
Although if I was brave enough
To fight my past
My past seemed a miraculous beauty
Where my mistakes have awakened me
And are still to warn me
There's none of your records
Even if it was you and your past
All this beauty is rising with time
Piling up lessons to preach in heaven
To the unborns Or the deads
Well my past wasn't me
But my older version
Full of unsafe and irrelevant stuffs and acts
And still am reverent for it
To secure my future
Years of unknown penance

And decade of building

Now are witnessing

The distinct versions of me

38. The fear of losing you

I would weave new days with you
I would recall my memories with you
That would be the most heart melting evidence
You would never investigate
It would be harder for you to watch
My tears of pain
May be you know I did a weep
But the heat of sympathy for me
Would be forever in me
Can't hold you but can feel pleasure
Memorizing that
Can't hear you but can talk to you virtually
You may not know you are the reason
And the goal of my life
And I can't ever think of losing you
I am here in front of you, do mark the
Most chaotic mind
I am dying fighting within myself
With regret and aspirations
With present and future
With past and memories
You may not know I am the most fearful person
I can't ever think of losing you…

39. Mind or mountain

The peak touches the sky
And its foot so deep and wide
Would I make mind to win its peak
Or the fear of height would let me abide
I dream of mountain so unreachable
But in dream I marked its defeat
I made up my mind to ignore its strength
And stepped gathering up my heat

40. While thinking of my imperfections

The morning so voracious
With the melodious vibes of chirpy
Little birds
And adding to the beauty was
My rise up
When the sun's rays glammed
Up my face
And I started my day, humming
Stability of my entire structure
Dancing gracefully
Happiness requires no step to learn
And dear me, unknowingly was
Vibing all along the beautiful day
As if it was the last day of my life
So reaching the mirror , I confidently
Made my head up
And no less than a blink of eye
I got non-plussed on this ugly dye
Indeed the mirror was reflecting me
So dark truth intangible, but need
No witness to last and packing up all
My imperfect beauty

I danced the most unstable one

Within so jaded

But couldn't pretend my glad

Poor me! That's the will of the nature

Wanding you this hopeless beauty

And in the dreams

When fairies were at far

Maybe the reason was my dark luster

I asked nature if it was unjust

And she didn't made a hesitation

To aware me to love the imperfect me

Love so deep that perfections fade off its beauty

And so was me

Not thinking but thanking my dark beauty

41. Beyond the old me

The day brighter like my devotion
And sun distanced as my destiny
I am a step before the threshold
That would indeed take me beyond the old me
Cause the time has turned me too young
To get on my hardworking days
Time is counting on my days to look for the modified me
Raising myself too above to obviate my nostalgic sense
Above the clouds to ignore the ground of dead leaves
A single person in dark crowd
Where every warmth and comfort trespasses
And I working like a labour of my dream
To reach that only vision
Not waiting but watching progress I am going through
Where for every hurt, Mom's veil is folded
And friend's sharing is splitting like marbles
The sea dead thinking for the grave like life ahead to
reach the heaven
Right, but bitter not the taste but the road
Taking me with intense ups and downs
Tragic losses that only I will bear
And still doubted for that single gem

42. This was my fate

Indeed for society I was a liability
Finding my indulgence in household only
For little mistakes, was condemned so brutal
Their mere perceptions biding me lonely.
Their superiority was tradition
A tradition laid in the curse of knowledge
They preferred prioritizing their entity
Discriminated females to hug this weigh
Since childhood, I was subjected to restrictions
Then to another world, was confined
Not a trace of opportunity permitted to my life door
And was ridiculously derided for lagging behind.
As per ritual, was departed from my beloved home
Where I had the most redolent childhood memories to
keep
the in-laws house, where my every step was fearful
Overwrought by nostalgia, got no tranquil sleep.
Accentuated as a member, but considered a burden
Unknowingly, I became the matter of their grief and rage
Feeling myself so suffocated within
This manly prepared exclusive cage
The scene turned wild when
I was taken as a puppet and played persistently

They used up my body cruelly until was emotionally dead
Mercilessly was thrown out of use, damaging me
physically and mentally
At such height, winds of loneliness fading off my soul
I had no care taker to wait
Yet empowering myself repeatedly to deal this challenge
Sadly, still they say "this was my fate"

43. Puppet of society

When born at a place
I was given a blank mind
Before this what the past was
I had no idea, I could not remind
A new life started
Days began counting my health
New to every thing around
I tried relishing every hold of my breath
She was my mom and a handsome dad
I was gradually being acquainted to many
Then was equipped with materialistic things
And asked for having aim any
I had a mind blocked and confined
Never was knowing life is one
Still unknown to the world outside
And far from the defeat and won
Ignoring this sphere, I was on routine
That all were tend to make
Parents are support in beginning
And we to soften life for their sake
So life to me seemed like a cycle
Then penetration paved in the books
Turning me practically zero

And at teenage focused on looks
That wasn't all I was motivated and forced
For pursuing a job to earn
Then was married to a girl honestly
Felt myself too prisoned to learn
They, roled as society, we're happy
Though involved complaining a bit
For their definition, now realizing, I have
Brutally spent without revealingly
And with dare enjoying any whit.

44. Regret burning alive

I was a fearsome, a troubling man to be
Cause nothing perfect adorned my life
I had been waiting for some occult such
So I would go without a pensive mind
In fact lifetime is short
Too short for my ambitions
Yet the little could be used as wanted
Cause, fault lies in my body
I was to get all snap clear and wide
And ignored all stupid and waste stuff aside
To be honest, I lost that pleasure
And still was abiding myself
To the busy schedule to console
For all the blames mounting above my head
The sleep of tranquility is never my reach
Cause I am not a happy soul either
I had been complaining all about
And would with an imaginary box of complains indeed
To check out this life, I had paid vast
Yet could not acquire the whole
At the end, I would sit lonely with just the soup bowl
And even if fortunate to get someone with me
I was in draft saving up all my consolations

Because I never befriended death to live life

45. Into the tears

The day brought fate, charming and smooth
And filled my heart and mind with enthusiasm
Adding colors to the surrounding bright
A day ahead I narrated with the same jump of heart
A year hence, with wide grin and lots of excitement
Ten years then, reminisced it like a picture in my album
Later in my life it became a memory of joy
At the end, the first smile of pride and bliss
Turned in tears of the lost memory

46. Meeting myself

One day or a night, in an unlisted sight
Standing afore with eyes bright and contacting
And I could position myself to the contact
Linking my mind direction to me, my confidence
Happiness unfolded and eyes recognized
It was me , no the aspiring me
A second later, eyes escaped giving way to red light
Surrounding our extremes
And vibing all set in my heart
Belief flourishing like a red carpet
On which walked my sole satisfaction and sacrifice
Linking myself to what I needed in my heart
What I made grief of was the redness so dull in me
And what it was set to be
Awaiting in the dark my love
Love that I showered
Not that I relished
And I met the core me, my base
Slipping through these, I crashed into my fear
But wasn't hurt, cause the best me had none of it
And this marked my line to be decorated after dizziness.

47. Deep breath of life

Green turns dull and decays being black
Into the soil it needed once to sprout
The death met my happiness and played gamble to deceive
My happiness so blessed raised light of defence
To this bad defeat, death penanced early morning and late night
To revert with the darkest light
To envelope the bliss of my life
And my life so unaware, played in the virtuality of joyous world
And the soul within, heard its feet trembling of my light
Stretched my arms to breathe the deepest and get into the best of me and my life
The deepest breath hugged the darkest light
And the conquest shivered the ground
Suspense washing off excites second by second
Favoring the conquest to the depth of my blessed life

48. Sharing the jewel

He sat so down
Turning like the soil on ground
Swinging like dead
On the laughing swing
Depression never laughs
It teases so inhuman
Sets up within the fire to end
And treads the thoughts under its weight
And all the symptoms in my mind
Matched with his position
And I made my mind
Not to help but to hesitate him
Made him feel more down
I stood up a fore
And danced strangely
Teasing the fate and
Enjoying its defamation
I laughed and danced again
Singing broken but melodious song
On spot sung by me
And he still disappointed
But raised his head
Asked me to stop this silly scene

Me, so ignorant resumed my tune

And he kept on stopping me

An hour later he forgot

In stopping me from the silly dance and song

Soon his happy hormone woke up

To meet me, stupid but funny

At the moment

Commanding his body and mind to company me

And he said happily

"I didn't know you came to defy my defeat"

"And deride my death"

49. Soulless

To the lady of this universe
Grandly adorned with vastness of stars
Shinning among the dazzling ways
Slow walk to guard and guide the existence
Meeting the guards of green minds
A humble touch is needed
To green the dried
And she being pensive
Of all excuses and carelessness
Cursed the planet dwellers
Of living a life of dry trees
Innocence sparkled of her raged eyes
Stone on heart and heaviness in voice
She kept on claiming the hurt to soulless
Speechless they, couldn't find guts to guilt
And shattered the pace of merciless cut
Climb and jump to the standing soul
They said lifeless and prioritized their soul
Of greed
The grapes that hugged the tiny twigs
And the nuts spreading on ground
Came to life on hearing the claim
Of the lady

Rose to the fullest voice of pain
Of the trees, flowers and wind
Of what they harmed so cruelly.

50. Sweat that awakes

The noon isn't cool near the pond
Nor the trees have shade to give
Their minds and body,
Weary of loads and hoards,
Of lots of work request to lay
Under the shaded but shadeless tree
Under the cloudy but burning sun
Near the cool but evaporating pond
On the green but pricking grass
Yet they, ignoring all these bad
Rested so peacefully on the aching land
There was no beauty yet seemed a folk
Their sweat of hard work peacefully awoke

51. Meet on death

Finally I met the river
I had drew water from
While I saw it
I believed that nothing has changed
But the grasses were dull
The trees were thirsty
The animals turned skinny
The people were sick
The sky turned bald
The clouds had ply
The houses were in ruin
Still the river flow so clear and fresh
I could find the river still alive
But the surrounding dead
The blues were yellow
And the dead was me

52. From crown to ground

Wiping his tears, he, trying to hide his pain
Pain of his dead bride about to leave
Her eye flickering like broken lamp
And tears off her shadow eyes
She knew it was for the last time
A full view of her beloved
Equipped with machines of breath
Life was being injected to lifeless
Body turned pale and skinny
Closing her forever closing eyes
She chose to met death being dead
And holding the hand of his
She persisted on the bed
For the first time, she had hold
Like a princess
Second, when felt the pain
And then scared to gain a feel
His touch could spare this drain
From first he had made feel
She is the crown of his life
And she shinning for loyalty and love
Forever was about to proceed in soil

53. The stars and me

The stars and me
Standing aloof and alone
With the time passing and leaves falling
The two separate distanced parallel
Desires still awaits us
For time lent no mercy
The moon guarding those
With vanishing strength and entity
Sometimes letting them face alone
Being hid under clouds
The mountains under the shine
Passing like never existed
But the numbers marked on my skin

54. The mermaid of dream

There is always a start
There is always a way
I don't thus mind
I don't thus care
For any such cape
Not a coward
Just blowing a escape
Not a coward
Just meeting a escape
I didn't want to land
The land of hope dwellers
I didn't want to eat
The food of satisfaction
First for all
I wanted grant of my action
And fire up my ambitions
Build up my drives
Suck up my fears
Such types of parallel world
I would rather fold up my arms
And pack up my mind to listen just me
Getting out of ice
Getting rid of fire

Getting off the rain

And breathing in pain

No complains up my shoulders

No dirt up on head

Me heading up to spread the

Drops of myself in rain

Waving my hair and thinking just a dark in shaking

Waiting up for rocks to break my ache

And me swaying like a mermaid in soft water with myself

no more fake

55. If mirror was a myth

If mirror was a myth
My beauty was blind
And their ugliness was vague
My guilt was false
Surviving without body
And eyes never wet for
Something unthought and untouched
View was their
And though ambiguous but judgements were facts
If mirror was a myth
My confidence was a brave knight massacred in the field
of doubt
And my love for myself was peacefully fading
No utterance for such biased motion
And my soul was never to climb a cliff
If mirror was a myth

56. Vague but value

Shiniest were the pearls
Floating away from the reach
Beyond the setting horizon
And disappearing of their vague impression marked the
time run
Which couldn't be captured
In the eyes dazzled by the light of pearls
Around the eyes and eyesight could meet those pearls
But poor were the hands
Tormenting for value
And guilty was the mind overthinking for the value
Unleashed were the abuses for the stupid fate
And brave was the heart to bear the loss

57. For the inclined climb

They are genius indeed
And I can't stop mocking at them
Their positivity is such inclined to well
They feel would bring them water
Dear me, they still incline so much
Craze, greed or need I fail to align
But lastly their hope brings them fall
And hope steps off the embankment
Like me mocking at them

58. Pleasure lying low

I never felt the winds at my feet
never the waves cascading my ankles
It never happened to see
the little ants tickling my toe
neither the grass soothing my sole
For no worry over my head
I never felt the comfort
of loose soil
Yet I feel down
Yet I feel low
Yet I never felt the pleasure
that was always lying low

59. The broken me

I broke a mirror
Thousand pieces apart
And made myself to see the broken me
Weird but my idea was smart
My eye on a piece
And lips on another
My hands were divided brutally
The shiniest me now seemed blur
I bent to uplift
My heart and eyes
The edge touched my tears
Reflecting my dark era of cries
Standing me wasn't suspicious
If the broken parts were broken me
They were laid on ground such
As if my ruins were waiting for sea

60. The dead head

Even if I walk away forever
My birds won't cry
My dogs won't weep
My flowers would never fade
Off their beauty
My pen would never sink in words
My family won't miss my presence
Adapted to the dead me
That can never force out of the buried soil

For your suggestions and reviews, you can connect to the writer on social media platforms :

1) Facebook (@sunlightraviyadav)

2) Instagram (@sunlightraviyadav).

3) Mail (sunlightraviyadav@gmail.com)

www.ingramcontent.com/pod-product-compliance
Lightning Source LLC
Chambersburg PA
CBHW021113130726
47988CB00003B/1000